MLA
Made Easy

Your Concise Guide
to the 9th Edition

Mark Hatala, Ph.D.

Greentop Academic Press • Greentop, Missouri

MLA Made Easy: Your Concise Guide to the 9th Edition
by Mark Hatala, Ph.D.

ISBN-13: 978-1-933167-60-2
ISBN-10: 1-933167-60-2

Book Design: Charles Dunbar

The font used in this book is Times New Roman, which is an approved font of the *MLA Handbook*; however, the interior uses a 10-point font to save space - MLA style requires a font between 11 and 13 points.

To incorporate this book into your classroom, visit our website at MLAcentral.com

Table of Contents

Why this book

I have written several books on writing, and this is my second book on MLA style. Why do I think that this book is needed? A couple of reasons.

First, the *MLA Handbook* has come out in a new 9th edition, so a new book is needed to cover changes from the previous edition.

Second, while the MLA publishes its own "official" handbook, it is 367 pages long! That is understandable because the book needs to cover just about every possible contingency, but it is NOT concise, in my opinion, for the typical student. Concise is 60 pages or less, not 367 pages or more. Also, the *MLA Handbook* uses no examples of student papers, which I find unhelpful. In my experience, students learn best when they have sample papers to provide context. Therefore, two heavily annotated student papers are included in this book!

Third, the other "brief" guides are all about formatting, not writing. A two-minute YouTube video can teach you all you need to know about formatting, but it takes a book to teach you how to write an MLA style paper.

Finally, I think that the other "brief" guides on the market are outdated crap. They often have instructions on how to format your paper using Microsoft Word (as if we live in 1998) and their "sample papers" look nothing like a regular paper in terms of margins and spacing. They don't even include YouTube, TED Talks, and social media as possible sources! They also provide no instruction on how to actually FIND academic sources.

Therefore, this book will guide you through the 9th edition of the *MLA Handbook* in a way that is brief, concise, and relevant to papers written in the 2020s (and beyond).

I have a number of videos explaining MLA style on both YouTube and my website, MLAcentral.com. The website brings together videos, supplements, worksheets, dozens of sample student papers, and just about anything else you would need to write a successful MLA style paper. So check it out.

You made the right (or "write") choice in buying this book.

Mark Hatala, Ph.D.
Professor of Psychology
Truman State University

Finding appropriate sources

You have your assignment - now what? First of all, congratulations! You've been given the opportunity to learn and be creative. However, now you need to find appropriate academic sources for your paper, and that search is going to start on the web.

Wikipedia

While using *Wikipedia* as a source in your paper tells your instructor "I didn't try, and I don't care," specific topics are backed up with cited research, and the citations are referenced at the bottom of the *Wikipedia* webpage. For example, a broad topic like "book censorship in the US" has 111(!) articles cited on *Wikipedia*, and these articles are literally a click away from being incorporated into your paper. Even a narrow topic like the "Three Witches" (characters in Shakespeare's *Macbeth*) has 33 cited articles. The earlier 8th edition of the *MLA Handbook* encouraged writers to "follow up on the sources that *Wikipedia* entries cite" (12), and I would agree.

Google Scholar (and just plain old Google)

Google Scholar (scholar.google.com) is an even broader database than *Wikipedia*. Google Scholar (and just plain old Google.com) also contains links to websites, full-text PDFs of academic articles, and other sources that provide the most up-to-date information for a particular topic. To use the previous examples again, "book censorship in the US" has 409,000 results in Google Scholar, and "Three Witches in *Macbeth*" has 31,400. That's a lot of information to sort through!

MLA database - *MLA International Bibliography*

If you are a college student (or if your school is affiliated with a university library), you will also have access to the *MLA International Bibliography*, which is an enormous online database for journals in the fields of language and literature. A problem with both *Wikipedia* and Google Scholar is that they often link to just a summary or abstract of an article. The *MLA International Bibliography* solves the access problem as it provides full-text access to over 1,000 journals, everything from *Applied Linguistics* to *Renaissance Quarterly*. If you require access to a journal article, you'll find it here!

Data mining from articles and books

The truth is that someone with a Ph.D. has already done your source search for you - the people who write articles and books. Authors of academic works cite the sources that are relevant to their topic, and these are easily found in the "works cited" section of a paper or book. This method is a gift that keeps on giving because it creates a positive feedback loop of published academics doing your work for you. It frees you from having to determine whether an article is "important" or not, and it provides a wide range of relevant articles to choose from. Your instructor will know what academic work is important, and by using this method to find articles, you won't be blindsided by them asking "Why didn't you use the most famous article on this topic in your paper?!"

The bottom line

I believe that incorporating all of the above methods is the best and most exhaustive way of finding appropriate sources for your paper. Even the previous edition of the *MLA Handbook* said that "Google and *Wikipedia* are reasonable places to begin your research" (12). My advice is to use *Wikipedia* to help clarify a topic that is interesting to you, then find more relevant articles using the full-text feature available through Google Scholar and if you have access to it, the MLA database. Next, use the articles you found to see what foundational work they cite. Then find those articles. In this way, all of your bases are covered - you'll have a variety of sources, from the foundational work to the most recent research on your topic.

Writing your paper

Now that you have collected and read all of your sources, you are ready to start writing! Academic papers tend to be very "dry" and to the point - just the facts - with little need to entertain the reader. MLA papers can seem "formulaic" and that is appropriate, because you are essentially writing according to a formula, with rules that are expected to be followed. The same kinds of things are expected in all academic papers - a review of the relevant literature, in-text citation of sources, the works cited page, etc. Departing from the formula does not make you creative so much as it makes you **wrong**. This is not to say that writing to a formula is easy. It is, however, very straightforward.

Here is a point that I cannot stress enough - write from an outline! The time it takes to write an outline is more than made up in the time it saves you when it comes time to write your paper. The outline doesn't have to be especially detailed, but should note the places you will write about different sources.

Every paper is different, but most follow a basic structure or "shape." The "shape" of the paper is like an hourglass - broad at the beginning, narrow in the middle, broad at the end. In other words, your paper should begin and end in fairly broad generalities, and discuss specific sources in the middle. This is where an outline comes in handy. It allows you to visualize how the different components - the opening, the sources, the in-text citations, quotations, and everything else - come together to form a complete paper.

In-text Citations

In-text citations get their own section because of the many problems they cause. It seems easy enough - you should use an in-text citation in your paper whenever you are paraphrasing, discussing someone else's ideas, or taking a quotation from another source. **Basically, when you're writing about someone else's work, it should be clear whose work it is that you're writing about**. If you're writing about your own thoughts, you don't need an in-text citation. When you start writing about someone else's, you need to give them attribution or credit. This allows the reader to then find the source in the works cited list and read it for themselves if they like.

One author

An example might make things clearer, and so here is one taken from the sample paper on *Macbeth* included at the end of this book. The same sentence, based on information from a journal article, can be rewritten several different ways:

Jajji asserts that "Lady Macbeth is ambitious, but her ambition brooks no barriers, moral or temporal" (234).

According to critics, Lady Macbeth has an ambition that "brooks no barriers, moral or temporal" (Jajji 234).

The idea that Lady Macbeth's ambition "brooks no barriers, moral or temporal" (Jajji 234), has been asserted by some critics.

Note: No punctuation is placed between the author's name and the page number.

Each sentence is providing the same basic information from page 234 of M. Ayub Jajji's journal article entitled "A Feminist Reading of Shakespearean Tragedies: Frailty, Thy Name is Woman." If the quotation took up two pages in the original work, a page span (e.g. 234-35) would be included in the citation.

While the examples involve a quotation, attribution should be provided whenever you are paraphrasing someone else's ideas too! For example:

Lady Macbeth is a character who is unobstructed by moral barriers (Jajji 234).

Finally, you should provide an in-text citation when discussing someone else's ideas. For example:

Ambition is at the core of Lady Macbeth's personality, and M. Ayub Jajji believes that she will stop at nothing to achieve her goals (234).

As you can see, the same basic idea (Lady Macbeth is ambitious) can be expressed through a number of different sentences. The same information can be presented via a quotation, or through paraphrasing, or even by discussing someone else's idea, but in each case, the original source is given attribution through an in-text citation.

Here is the citation of the article as it would appear on the works cited page:

Jajji, M. Ayub. "A Feminist Reading of Shakespearean Tragedies: Frailty, Thy Name is Woman." *Pakistan Journal of Commerce and Social Sciences*, vol. 8, no. 1, 2014, pp. 228-37.

Two authors

But what if a citation has two authors? In that case, BOTH are included in the in-text citation! Here's an example from a paper on the efficacy of napping:

Tietzel, Amber J., and Leon C. Lack. "The Recuperative Value of Brief and Ultra-Brief Naps on Alertness and Cognitive Performance." *Journal of Sleep Research*, vol. 11, no. 3, 2002, pp. 213-18, https://doi.org/10.1046/j.1365-2869.2002.00299.x.

Sleep researchers Amber Tietzel and Leon Lack found that even a short nap (10 minutes) resulted in improved alertness (216).

Sleep researchers have found that even a short nap (10 minutes) resulted in improved alertness (Tietzel and Lack 216).

Sleep researchers have found that even a short nap (10 minutes) resulted in "significantly improved alertness and cognitive performance" (Tietzel and Lack 216).

Three or more authors

Citation is just as easy when there are three or more authors. Just list the first author and "et al." (meaning "and others"). For example:

Akehurst, Lucy, et al. "Effect of Socially Encountered Misinformation and Delay on Children's Eyewitness Testimony." *Psychiatry, Psychology and Law*, vol. 16, no. 1, 2009, pp. 125-36, https://doi.org/10.1080/13218710802620406.

Lucy Akehurst and colleagues have found that suggestibility is higher in children when misinformation is presented in a social context (134).

Researchers have found that suggestibility is higher in children when misinformation is presented in a social context (Akehurst et al. 134).

One-page works

If a source is only one page (like an editorial, magazine, or newspaper article), then you don't have to put the page number in an in-text citation. For example:

Weinberger, Eric. "Off the Reservation." *The New York Times*, 15 June 2003, p. G13.

Critic Eric Weinberger points out that Alexie "works under the strain most other writers don't, as an Indian writer, or maybe an important Indian writer, or at least the important Indian writer of the moment."

Website with an author (and no page numbers)

What if you are using a source from a website? Websites don't have page numbers, and so no number should be provided in the in-text citation. Earlier editions of MLA style would include the paragraph number that the information is taken from (you would actually count the unnumbered paragraphs), but this is no longer neccessary in the 9th edition. Here's an example from the *Macbeth* sample paper:

Like the Weird Sisters, Lady Macbeth is also portrayed as "harsh and crazy" (Donkor).

Donker, Michael. "Character Analysis: Lady Macbeth." *British Library*, 19 May 2017, www.bl.uk/shakespeare/articles/character-lady-macbeth.

Work with no identifiable author (or page numbers)

What if you're using a source that doesn't have an identified author (or page numbers)? In this case, use the title of the work in the citation. Here is an example, also from the *Macbeth* sample paper:

The Weird Sisters are the first characters introduced in the play and are also the first to foreshadow the demise of Macbeth ("Three Witches").

An in-text citation is used here because the idea expressed in the sentence is paraphrasing information taken from *Wikipedia*. While some teachers are fine with their students using *Wikipedia* as a source in a paper, others are not, so be sure to ask whether it is acceptable before you start writing your paper!

YouTube, TED Talk, video lecture, or podcast

What if you're using a source from a video lecture or podcast? In this case, the in-text citation would include a time stamp - the hour, minute, and second (or seconds) of the source that you are using in your paper. Again, let's return to the *Macbeth* sample paper, which includes an in-text citation of a YouTube video.

However, in Shakespearean literature, an essential element is the female persona as being predominantly viewed in a "negative, helpless, or evil way" (Solomon 00:01:33-38).

This sentence is quoting information that was presented between minute 1:33-1:38 in a YouTube video entitled "Feminist Analysis of Macbeth" created by Bersabbe Solomon.

Lines from a play (or poem)

I'll finish this section with an example of how you would write an in-text citation of lines from a play:

As Shakespeare writes, Lady Macbeth proclaims, "Come, you spirits / That tend on mortal thoughts, unsex me here, / And fill me from the crown to the toe top-full / Of direst cruelty / ... Come to my woman's breasts / And take my milk for gall, you murd'ring ministers ..." (*Macbeth* 1.5.47-55).

Those are some powerful words (I love *Macbeth* and see it performed live every chance I get)! The in-text citation refers to the fact that the lines from the play come from Act 1, Scene 5, lines 47-55 (abbreviated down to 1.5.47-55). Roman numerals (or whatever numbering system is used in the original work) used to be acceptable, but MLA now prefers the use of Arabic numerals when providing this information.

The Works Cited Page

Sources are cited in MLA style so that a reader can find the same work if they are so inclined, and the *MLA Handbook* discusses the "core elements" that should appear (and the ORDER they should appear) for a source in any works cited list. I believe that it is easier to understand these "core elements" in the context of actual examples, and it's important to remember that every citation won't contain all (or even most) of the "core elements." I outline them here (including the punctuation that follows each) as an aid to understanding why elements of a citation are in the order they're in:

1. **Author.** - This is the creator of the work, and could be a writer, artist, group, or organization. Individuals are presented last name first, then the full first name (and middle initial, if provided). For multiple (and anonymous) authors of the work, see the examples below.

2. **Title of source.** - The title is placed in quotation marks if it's part of a bigger piece of work (like a chapter in a book or an episode of a television series). It is italicized if it is "self-contained" (like a whole book, or collection of poetry, or entire television series). If there is no title for a work, a description is provided (e.g. marble sculpture).

3. **Title of container,** - A container is what holds the source you are using in your paper. So, if the source is an online video on YouTube, then YouTube is the container. Similarly, a newspaper (like the *New York Times* or *Wall Street Journal*) is the container for a newspaper article, and a journal is the container of a journal article.

4. **Contributors,** - This can refer to everything from the directors of movies to the translators of books to the performers in a play. Sometimes they're listed, sometimes not, depending on the context and the focus of the paper.

5. **Version,** - For some sources, it's important to know the version used. For example, the Bible could be presented in the King James version (KJV), the New International version (NIV), the Christian Standard version (CSB), and about a dozen others. The reader should know what version you used in your paper.

6. **Number,** - This could refer to a volume and/or issue number for a journal or the season and episode number for a television series.

7. **Publisher,** - This could be something obvious, like the publisher of a book, or something less obvious, like the studio that produces movies or television series.

8. **Publication date,** - The same source is sometimes published at different times in different mediums. For example, a magazine or newspaper article could come out earlier on the magazine or newspaper's website. You would report the

publication date of the source you used, usually in the format of date, month (abbreviated), and year (20 Dec. 2019).

9. **Location.** - This is a "jargony" way of saying page numbers. So a newspaper article might appear in section C, page 3 of a physical newspaper, and be cited as "p. C4" (but not in quotes!). If a source takes up multiple pages (like in a book or a journal), it is preceded by "pp." (pp. 34-63). For performances viewed in person (such as a play or concert), the location is where the performance took place. For websites and sources located in a digital network, URLs and DOIs are provided (see examples below).

Supplemental Elements. - The date the information was accessed is included in a citation where there is no date provided for when the information was posted or if the source has been altered or changed. This information is provided at the end of the citation in the form of date, month, and year (Accessed 31 Oct. 2021.)

A note about the number of authors

As can be seen in the "core elements" above, the author of a source comes first in a citation. If there is only one author, they are listed last name first, then a comma, then the rest of their name (as presented in the source). For example, my favorite book of all time is Ernest Hemingway's *The Sun Also Rises*, and the original print edition would be cited as:

Hemingway, Ernest. *The Sun Also Rises*. Scribners, 1926.

What about a source with TWO authors? The first author is listed the same way (last name first), but the second author is written out as you would normally write a name (first name first). Here's an example of the famous book by the *Washington Post* journalists who broke the story about the Watergate break-in that brought down President Nixon in 1972:

Bernstein, Carl, and Bob Woodward. *All the President's Men*. Simon & Schuster, 1974.

What about a source with THREE OR MORE authors? While this would be more common with a journal article or a translation, I'd like to use a book example with three authors to keep things congruent. But who writes a book with two other people?

Well, in 2016, three *New York Times* bestselling authors, Karen White, Beatriz Williams, and Lauren Willig worked together to release a historical fiction novel called *The Forgotten Room*. As you can see in the example below, things simplify quite a bit when a source has three or more authors, with the first author listed (last name first) followed by the phrase "et al." (which means "and others"):

White, Karen, et al. *The Forgotten Room*. Penguin, 2016.

Note: The same rules apply to every other type of work with multiple authors.

Works Cited Page Examples

There are so many permutations for different types of sources. Because of that, much of this book is made up of examples of the type of sources you're likely to encounter and use in your own paper. While the *MLA Handbook* doesn't use these explicit groupings, I've found it helpful to think of sources as being classified as **written works** (journal articles, books, book chapters, etc.), **audiovisual media** (podcasts, YouTube videos, photographs, you name it), and **online media** (websites, tweets, and social media). All citations contain pretty much the same information (see the previous two pages), but the way they are presented can be slightly different, depending on the context and focus of the paper. I've also made an effort to show how the *same* source is cited, depending on how it was obtained (e.g. in a book, online, on a streaming service).

Written Works

Books (including Kindle, e-book, and audiobook editions)

Books are a useful source of information when you're writing a paper, especially if the assignment is to write a paper about that book! A generic example of a book reference is a little silly without context, so here's an actual book citation (of another book I love, Harper Lee's *To Kill a Mockingbird*), and then all of the permutations:

Lee, Harper. *To Kill a Mockingbird.* Harper, 1960.

But what if you bought the Kindle version (an e-book) off of Amazon? That would look pretty similar:

Lee, Harper. *To Kill a Mockingbird.* Kindle ed., HarperCollins, 2014.

What if you choose instead to listen to the book rather than read it? The audiobook narrated by actress Sissy Spacek would be a good option! Again, it looks similar:

Lee, Harper. *To Kill a Mockingbird.* Narrated by Sissy Spacek, audiobook ed., HarperAudio, 2014.

Taking the citations apart, the "core elements" are present - the name of the author, the title of the book, the edition (if applicable, to denote that it's an e-book, a Kindle, or audiobook edition), the publisher, and the year of publication.

But why read or listen to the book?! I've heard the movie is pretty good! That's a joke, and you should definitely read (or listen to) the book, but if you DID watch the movie, the citation would look like:

To Kill a Mockingbird. Directed by Robert Mulligan, Universal Pictures, 1962.

The citation of an e-book format is similar to that of a Kindle edition. To make things more meta, here is the e-book citation for the 9th edition of the *MLA Handbook*:

MLA Handbook. 9th ed., e-book ed., Modern Language Association of America, 2021.

Book in translation

I was a Russian major as an undergraduate, and so had the opportunity to read a number of the classics of Russian literature. However, my Russian was not THAT good, so the books were all in translation. For example:

Tolstoy, Leo. *War and Peace*. Translated by Richard Pevear and Larissa Volokhonsky, Vintage, 2008.

I also teach classes in psychology, but when I read Freud, it is in translation. Sometimes the translator also takes on a second role, and so that should also appear in the citation, as in:

Freud, Sigmund. *The Interpretation of Dreams: The Complete and Definitive Text*. Edited and translated by James Strachey, 1st ed., Basic Books, 2010.

Book without an author

What about a book like *Beowulf*? Who knows who wrote that Anglo-Saxon epic? Rather than list "Anonymous" as the author, you would just begin with the title of the book, then list who did the translation, then the publisher, and then the year of publication:

Beowulf. Translated by Seamus Heaney, Farar, Straus, and Giroux, 2000.

Note: I can't recommend the movie they made of *Beowulf*, so I won't provide a citation if it.

The Bible

If you're using the Bible as a source, it's important to make clear which version you are using. Even though it's the Bible, it still has a publisher too!

The Bible. Authorized King James Version. Robert Carroll and Stephen Prickett, editors, Oxford UP, 1998.

Note: The publisher, Oxford University Press, can be abbreviated to "Oxford UP."

What if you are not reading a physical copy of the Bible, but instead reading it on your phone and accessing it through an app? The King James version would look like:

The Bible. King James Version. *Bible Gateway*, version 42, Bible Gateway / Zondervan, 2016. App.

Note: The advantage of using an app such as Bible Gateway is that you are able to access over 30 different versions of the Bible, including the New King James Version (NKJV), the International Standard Version (ISV), and the New Living Translation (NLT). Just be sure to make it clear which version you are using!

Book chapters, essays, forewords, prefaces, etc.

MLA style doesn't draw much of a distinction between a chapter in an edited book and the foreword from the same book, but you're MUCH more likely to use the former in your papers. Book chapters are treated as a hybrid of a book and a journal because books, like journals, have editors. Journals have editors too, but they're not listed in the citation. Why? Who knows? Again, it's unclear, so here's an example of a book chapter:

Freese, Peter. "Kurt Vonnegut's *Slaughterhouse-Five*, or How to Storify an Atrocity." *Historiographic Metafiction in Modern American and Canadian Literature*, edited by Bernard Engler and Kurt Muller, Schoningh Paderborn, 1994, pp. 209-22.

All of the "core elements" are present - the name of the author, the title of the chapter, the title of the book (in italics), the editors who compiled the book, the publisher, the year of publication, and the page numbers of the chapter.

Comic books and graphic novels

If you are a fan of jargon, comic books and graphic novels are, according to MLA style, *graphic narratives*. For citation purposes, they are often (but not always) numbered. I've included examples of the first Spider-Man comic and the first appearance of Superman (in an anthology of stories called *Action Comics*).

Lee, Stan, and Steve Ditko. *The Amazing Spider-Man*, no. 1, Marvel Comics, 1963.

Siegel, Jerry, and Joe Schuster. "Superman." *Action Comics*, no. 1, National Allied Publications, 1938, pp. 1-13.

Note: An original *Action Comics* sold on eBay in 2014 for over three million dollars!

Graphic novels are cited in the same way as books:

Satrapi, Marjane. *Persepolis: The Story of a Childhood*, Pantheon Graphic Library, 2004.

The movie version would be cited as:

Persepolis. Directed by Vincent Paronnaud and Marjane Satrapi, Sony Pictures Classics, 2007.

Dictionary - in print or online

For general spelling, MLA style advises to pick one dictionary and stick with it, such as the *Merriam-Webster Collegiate Dictionary*. However, a number of very poor papers include the phrase "Webster's defines _____ as _____ ." as if they were giving a speech and believe a dictionary is an appropriate source for a paper. With that said, here is how you would cite a dictionary entry for the word "memory" (if you REALLY had to) - note that the "*N.*" in italics after the entry indicates that memory is a noun in the context of the paper.

In print:

"Memory, *N.* (1)." *Merriam-Webster's Collegiate Dictionary*, 11th ed., Merriam-Webster, 2019, p. 503.

Online:

"Memory, *N.* (1)." *Merriam-Webster*, 2021, merriam-webster.com/dictionary/memory.

Note: The word being defined is followed by how it is being used in italics ("*N.*" for noun, "*Adj.*" for adjective, etc.) and the number of the definition being used in parentheses (eg. 1, 2, 3, etc.). Although there was a time when every home contained a dictionary (and a set of encyclopedias) this has grown increasingly rare. My recommendation, if you're going to use a dictionary, is to use the online edition.

Doctoral dissertations and masters theses

These are sources that you are unlikely to use in your paper, but you may run across them while conducting a search of online databases. Doctoral dissertations are identified as such at the end of the citation, and the title of the work is in *italics*. Unpublished doctoral dissertations are usually "unpublished" for a reason, and so you probably won't use them as a source.

Hatala, Mark. *A Test of the Additive Unique-Features Model Using Consumer Product Preferences*. 1993. Ohio University, PhD dissertation.

Note: This is my actual dissertation and it has a $20 bill taped to the title page. The last time I visited it in Ohio University's Alden Library (in 2004), the $20 was still there.

Edited book

You might cite an entire edited book rather than a specific component (as in an anthology). In this case, identify the editor in your citation:

Oates, Joyce Carol, editor. *The Oxford Book of American Short Stories*. Oxford UP, 2012.

Government publications

While these are much more specialized sources, you may need to incorporate a Supreme Court decision or international treaty into a paper to show that you REALLY know what you're talking about. Examples follow:

Supreme Court cases

United States, Supreme Court. *Brown v. Board of Education. United States Reports*,
      vol. 347, 17 May 1954, pp. 483-97. *Library of Congress*, tile.loc.gov/storage-
      services/service/ll/usrep/usrep347/usrep347483/usrep347483.pdf.

United States, Supreme Court. *Plessy v. Ferguson. United States Reports*, vol. 167, 18
      May 1896, pp. 537-64. *Library of Congress*, tile.loc.gov/storage-services/
      service/ll/usrep/usrep163/usrep163537/usrep163537.pdf.

United States, Supreme Court. *Roe v. Wade. United States Reports*, vol. 410, 22
      Jan. 1973, pp. 113-78. *Library of Congress*, tile.loc.gov/storage-services/
      service/ll/usrep/usrep410/usrep410113/usrep410113.pdf.

Note: The Library of Congress is an excellent resource for full-text PDFs of rulings by the Supreme Court. The three examples here are monumental in the history of the United States, with *Brown v. Board of Education* overturning the "separate but equal" statutes of *Plessy v. Ferguson*, and *Roe v. Wade* creating a Constitutional "right to privacy."

Executive orders

United States, Executive Office of the President [Joe Biden]. Executive Order 14028:
      Improving the Nation's Cybersecurity. 12 May 2021. *Federal Register*, vol. 86,
      no. 93, 17 May 2021, pp. 22633-47, www.gpo.gov/content/pkg/FR-2021-05-
      17/pdf/2021-10460.pdf.

Treaties

Kyoto Protocol to the United Nations Framework Convention on Climate Change. United
      Nations, 1998, unfccc.int/resource/docs/convkp/kpeng.pdf. Multilateral treaty.

Journal articles - in print or online

      A generic example of a journal citation would be pretty meaningless, so here's an actual one, and then a breakdown of the component parts:

Isaacs, Neil D. "Unstuck in Time: *Clockwork Orange* and *Slaughterhouse-Five*."
      Literature/Film Quarterly, vol. 1, no. 2, 1973, pp. 122-31.

      That would be the citation if you had the physical print journal. If you accessed the journal online (after a Google Scholar search), you would include that retrieval information too, so it would look like:

Isaacs, Neil D. "Unstuck in Time: *Clockwork Orange* and *Slaughterhouse-Five*."
      Literature/Film Quarterly, vol. 1, no. 2, 1973, pp. 122-31. *JSTOR*, www.jstor.
      org/stable/43795411.

It's the same article either way, but accessed through different media (print vs. online). The most important thing is that the "core elements" are present - the name of the author, the title of the article, the name of the journal (in italics), the volume and number of the journal, and the page numbers of the source. The only difference is that if the article is accessed online, you would include information on how to find it through the *JSTOR* "permalink" (which is where a source is stored permanently in a digital network).

Note: *JSTOR* is a digital library started in 1995 and is short for "Journal Storage."

Similarly, DOI (digital object identifier) numbers have become pretty standard for journals since they were introduced in 2000. If a DOI is provided, put it at the end of the citation with the full "https://doi.org/" and number information:

Woertman, Liesbeth, and Femke van den Brink. "Body Image and Female Sexual
Functioning and Behavior: A Review." *The Journal of Sex Research*, vol. 49,
no. 2-3, 2012, pp. 184-211, https://doi.org/10.1080/00224499.2112.658586.

Note: Why do DOI numbers have to be so long?! Why isn't there a service to shorten them? Well, there is! Just go to the website provided by the International DOI Foundation (http://shortdoi.org) and plug the long DOI into their "shortener." For example, the above "https://doi.org/10.1080/00224499.2112.658586" shortens to "https://doi.org/d5zd." Why not just use the shortened DOIs in the original publication? It's a mystery to me.

While the previous examples have all been printed in a physical journal (even if they are accessed online), there are also journals which are entirely online, with no print edition. For example:

Holobut, Agata, and Jan Rybicki. "The Stylometry of Film Dialogue: Pros and Pitfalls."
Digital Humanities Quarterly, vol. 14, no. 4, 2020, www.digitalhumanities.org/
dhq/vol/14/4/000498/000498.html.

Magazine article - in print or online

You might decide to use a magazine article to provide some "pop culture" or "edgy" material to your paper. Here is how you would cite a magazine article, in this case an article about the cultural importance of the television show *Sex and the City*:

In print:
Armstrong, Jennifer Keishin. "*Sex and the City* and Us: How Four Single Women Changed
the Way We Think, Live, and Love." *Entertainment Weekly*, 11 May 2018,
pp. 32-5.

Online:
Armstrong, Jennifer Keishin. "*Sex and the City* and Us: How Four Single Women Changed
the Way We Think, Live, and Love." *Entertainment Weekly*, 5 May 2018, www.
ew.com/article/2018/05/05/sex-and-the-city-and-us.

You may notice that the dates are different on the "in print" and "online" editions of the same article. Both are actually correct, and my guess is that for *Entertainment Weekly*, information appears on their website before it appears in print. Or who knows? Print media is dead anyway.

Additionally, if you just wanted to cite the book itself rather than a magazine article about it, the book citation would look like this:

Armstrong, Jennifer Keishin. *Sex and the City and Us: How Four Single Women Changed the Way We Think, Live, and Love*. Simon & Schuster, 2018.

Newspaper article - in print or online

Newspapers can be a more up-to-date source for a particular topic. Here is how a citation looks for a newspaper article on agoraphobia:

In print:
Lukits, Ann. "Fear of Open Spaces May Be Linked to Animal Instincts." *The Wall Street Journal*, 19 Sept. 2016, p. D4.

Note: "D4" refers to the page number the article appeared on in the physical newspaper.

Online:
Lukits, Ann. "Fear of Open Spaces May Be Linked to Animal Instincts." *The Wall Street Journal*, 19 Sept. 2016, www.wsj.com/articles/fear-of-open-spaces-may-be-linked-to-animal-instincts-1474290002.

Newspaper editorial

Editorial Board. "Elizabeth Warren Tells the Truth." *The Wall Street Journal*, 16 May 2021, www.wsj.com/articles/elizabeth-warren-tells-the-truth-11621195472.

Strassel, Kimberly A. "Smiling at Corruption." *The Wall Street Journal*, 18 Oct. 2018, www.wsj.com/news/author/kimberly-a-strassel?page=13.

Note: Newspaper editorials follow the same citation structure as newspaper articles; however, sometimes they are written by individual authors and other times by the "Editorial Board" of the newspaper.

Plays and anthologies (Shakespeare and otherwise)

William Shakespeare's work has been available since the *First Folio* was published 1623 (seven years after his death), so there are a number of ways to obtain access to his great works. Here are three examples of *Hamlet*: a book of just the play, a Shakespeare anthology book (which contains ALL of his work), and online.

Shakespeare, William. *Hamlet*. Dover, 2017.

Shakespeare, William. "Hamlet." *An Oxford Anthology of Shakespeare*, edited by Stanley Wells. Oxford UP, 1991, pp. 306-99.

Shakespeare, William. "Hamlet." *The Folger Shakespeare*, www.shakespeare.folger.edu/shakespeares-works/hamlet.

Poetry book

A book of poetry would be cited the same way as any other book! Here is an example that includes Sonnet 43 ("How do I love thee? Let me count the ways.") from Elizabeth Barrett Browning:

Browning, Elizabeth Barrett. *Sonnets from the Portuguese: A Celebration of Love.* St. Martin's Press, 2007.

Another common occurrence is when you need to cite an individual poem from an anthology. Seventeenth century poet Anne Bradstreet's poem "The Author to Her Book" would be cited as:

Bradstreet, Anne. "The Author to Her Book." *The Oxford Book of American Poetry*, edited by David Lehman and John Brehm, 1st ed., Oxford UP, 2006, p. 3.

Oftentimes the easiest way to find a particular poem is online. Organizations like the Poetry Foundation are free, and make it easy to find the work you want. For example, the citation for Walt Whitman's 1892 version of "Song of Myself" would appear as:

Whitman, Walt. "Song of Myself (1892 version)." *Poetry Foundation*, www.poetryfoundation.org/poems/45477/song-of-myself-1892-version.

Press release

Press releases can be good sources because they present the most up-to-date information available. The problem is that if you're citing a press release from several years ago, the material might already be dated or incorrect. So, unless the press release has been issued within the past year, I would avoid including it in your paper. Here's an example from 2020:

"People Prone to Disengage From Difficult Tasks and Goals May Experience Greater Cognitive Decline After Retirement." *American Psychological Association*, 16 Mar. 2020, www.apa.org/news/press/releases/2020/03/cognitive-decline-retirement. Press release.

Reviews

Review of *The Dating Playbook*, by Farrah Rochon. *Kirkus Reviews*, 17 Aug. 2021, www.kirkusreviews.com/book-reviews/farrah-rachon/the-dating-playbook-rochon.

Szalai, Jennifer. "*Dedicated* Makes the Case for Choosing Something and Sticking With It." *The New York Times*, 12 May 2021, p. C4.

Varadarajan, Tunku. "*The Story of Yoga* Review: More Than Striking a Pose." *The Wall Street Journal*, 16 Apr. 2021, www.wsj.com/articles/the-story-of-yoga-review-more-than-striking-a-pose-11587078703.

Note: Reviews (of books, movies, performances, etc.) are sometimes titled and/or written by an identified reviewer, and sometimes not. Versions of both appear above (along with "in print" and online).

Audiovisual Media

Lots of great information can be gleaned from YouTube, paintings, TED Talks, live performances, interviews, or podcasts, and MLA style tells us how to cite it!

Art - Painting, Sculpture, or Photograph (really, ANY image)

I'm not so worldly that I wasn't moved when I saw the *Mona Lisa* in the Louvre, but I honestly didn't understand the fuss! There were plenty of other outstanding works of art that lacked the crowd that the *Mona Lisa* always seems to attract. However, you don't have to go to Paris to see the *Mona Lisa*, and your citation depends on how you have experienced it:

Viewed in person
Da Vinci, Leonardo. *Mona Lisa*. 1503, Musee du Louvre, Paris.

Viewed online
Da Vinci, Leonardo. *Mona Lisa*. 1503. Musee du Louvre, www.louvre.fr/en/oeuvre-notices/mona-lisa-portrait-lisa-gherardini-wife-francesco-del-giocondo.

Viewed in a book
Da Vinci, Leonardo. *Mona Lisa*. 1503. Musee du Louvre. *Leonardo da Vinci: The Complete Paintings in Detail*, by Alessandro Vezzosi, Prestel, 2019, p. 265.

If you're in Paris, you might as well hit all the big museums, and the small ones too! Want to see Rodin's *The Thinker*? It's outside, in the courtyard of the Rodin Museum.

Viewed in person
Rodin, Auguste. *The Thinker*. 1903, Musee Rodin, Paris. Bronze sculpture.

Viewed online
Rodin, Auguste. *The Thinker*. 1903. Musee Rodin, www.musee-rodin.fr/en/collections/sculptures/thinker-0.

Viewed in a book

Rodin, Auguste. *The Thinker*. 1903. Musee Rodin. *Rodin*, by Antoinette Le Normand-
    Romain, Abbeville Press Publishers, 2014, p. 91.

Note: As you can see, the name of the artist comes first, followed by the name of the work (in italics), then the museum where it is kept (and the city where the museum is located if seen in person), and how you accessed the image (if not in person). Adding supplemental information such as "bronze sculpture" is optional.

Film or movie (and what's the difference?)

I'm a big fan of Mozart, and so his 1980s biopic gets to be the "film" example.

Amadeus. Directed by Milos Forman, Orion Pictures, 1984.

If you watch it on the Netflix app, it would appear as:

Amadeus. Orion Pictures, 1984. *Netflix* app.

If you want to specifically emphasize the Oscar-nominated contributions of actors F. Murray Abraham and Tom Hulce (as a focus of discussion in your paper), the citation would look like:

Amadeus. Directed by Milos Forman, performances by F. Murray Abraham and Tom
    Hulce, Orion Pictures, 1984.

Note: Although both lead actors were nominated, the Oscar went to F. Murray Abraham.

Music song or album and music video

Album

Vampire Weekend. *Father of the Bride*. Columbia, 2019.

Song

Vampire Weekend. "This Life." *Father of the Bride*, Columbia, 2019. *Spotify* app.

Now you can judge me on my taste in music, but I need an example, so I'm going to use something that I like. The group or individual artist comes first in the citation, followed by the song (in quotation marks, if you're talking about a specific song), the name of the album (in italics), the record company, and the year of release. In this example, *Spotify* is the "container," but it could easily be another streaming service. If you wanted to cite the music video of the song (where the "container" is YouTube), it would be cited as follows:

Vampire Weekend. "This Life." *YouTube*, 20 May 2019, www.youtube.com/watch?v
    =FwkrrU2WYKg.

Note: Since the name of the group is the same as the "uploader," Vampire Weekend only needs to be cited once.

Concert

What about a concert by the band? Here is an example of a Vampire Weekend concert in Cleveland at the Jacobs Pavillion in support of their *Father of the Bride* album.

Vampire Weekend. *Father of the Bride Tour.* 14 June 2019, Jacobs Pavillion at Nautica, Cleveland.

Note: If you want to know what Vampire Weekend lead singer Ezra Koenig is going to look like in 30 years, flip to the back cover and take a look at my picture.

Performance (Play, Concert, Ballet, you name it)

This citation structure works for any public performance, but as I've said elsewhere in this book, I'm a big fan of Shakespeare's *Macbeth*, and this was the most recent time I saw it. It was a wonderful student production at Truman State University, where I'm a faculty member:

Shakespeare, William. *Macbeth*. Directed by David Charles Goyette, 13 Nov. 2019, James G. Severns Theater, Kirksville, Missouri.

What about a concert performance by individual artists? Here are examples from Nicki Minaj and Snoop Dogg concerts:

Minaj, Nicki. *The Nicki Wrld Tour.* 21 Feb. 2019, Olympiahalle, Munich, Germany.

Snoop Dogg. *Puff, Puff Pass Tour.* 29 Sept. 2001, American Airlines Arena, Miami.

Note: Proper spelling and punctuation are sometimes victims of artistic license. Nicki Minaj chose "Wrld" rather than "World" for her tour name, and Snoop Dogg should have an Oxford or serial comma after the second "Puff" (e.g. *Puff, Puff, Pass Tour*).

What about a comedian? I love Jim Gaffigan, so here is an example of a live comedy performance:

Gaffigan, Jim. *The Fun Tour*. 6 Aug. 2021, Encore Theater at Wynn, Las Vegas.

What about a ballet? You would have to build a time machine to witness this performance of *The Dying Swan* by Anna Pavlova:

Pavlova, Anna. *The Dying Swan*. Performance by the Ballets Russes, 11 Oct. 1905, Mariinsky Theatre, St. Petersburg, Russia.

Note: This was Anna Pavlova's most famous role - one that she choreographed herself.

Personal interviews

Part of my Quantified Self (QS) research used to involve working with lifeloggers (people who track every aspect of their lives), so there were a lot of personal interviews. If you conducted the interview, you don't need to put your name in the citation, and should cite the name of the person you interviewed, the modality of the interview (telephone, Skype, Zoom), and the date. For example:

Robinson, Ariq. Skype interview with the author. 11 Nov. 2016.

Podcast

Like many people, podcasts have replaced radio in my life. I still haven't had occasion to cite a podcast, but if you had to, this is how you would do it:

"The 10 best jobs in America." *Animal Spirits* from A Wealth of Common Sense, hosted by Ben Carlson and Michael Batnick, podcast ed., www.awealthofcommonsense. com/2020/01/animal-spirits-the-10-best-jobs-in-america. Accessed 15 Jan. 2021. MP3 format.

Note: This is a podcast about personal finance that I like quite a bit.

TED Talks (and online lectures and speeches)

The interesting thing about TED Talks (although there are MANY interesting things about them) is that they are cited differently based on whether they are watched on YouTube or the TED website (although they might appear on both)!

Confused? Me too! For example, social psychologist Amy Cuddy has a very interesting TED Talk on body language and how it impacts how people view us, as well as how we view ourselves. If you watch it on YouTube, the upload date is different from the TED site and YouTube is the "container." The citation looks like:

Cuddy, Amy. "Your Body Language May Shape Who You Are." *YouTube*, uploaded by TED, 1 Oct. 2012, www.youtube.com/watch?v=Ks-_Mh1QhMc&t=328s.

However, if the exact same video is viewed on the TED website, the citation would look like:

Cuddy, Amy. "Your Body Language May Shape Who You Are." *TED,* June 2012, www. ted.com/talks/amy_cuddy_your_body_language_may_shape_who_you_ are?language=en.

Why?! Basically, it comes down to the "container" the information is presented in. The video premiered on the TED website first (in June 2012) and was later added to YouTube (1 Oct. 2012) on the TED channel. This can be confusing, because the same information can be cited differently, but it has an internal logic if you think about it. But maybe it's best NOT to think about it.

Television show - series or individual episode

I'm a huge fan of *Arrested Development*, which is not particularly surprising given my demographic profile. If you wanted to focus on the creator Mitchell Hurwitz and cite the entire series as it appeared on Fox television, it would look like this:

Hurwitz, Mitchell, creator. *Arrested Development*. Imagine Television, The Hurwitz Company, and Twentieth Century Fox Television, 2003-2006.

But what about an individual episode? In my opinion "Beef Consomme" is one of the best episodes, where the characters try to find a guy named "Hermano" because they don't realize that it is Spanish for "brother." Why would you include an episode of *Arrested Development* in your paper? Good question!

The "container" that you use to access *Arrested Development* is meaningful, so HOW you watch it requires modifying the citation accordingly.:

Viewed on a streaming service, website, or app
"Beef Consomme." Directed by Jay Chandrasekhar. *Arrested Development*, created by Mitchell Hurwitz, season 1, episode 13, Imagine Television, The Hurwitz Company, and Twentieth Century Fox Television, 15 Feb. 2004. *Netflix*, www.netflix.com.

Note: If you viewed the episode on the Amazon Prime app, instead of "Netflix" at the end of the citation, you would put: *Amazon Prime Video* app.

Viewed on a DVD
"Beef Consomme." 2004. *Arrested Development: Season One,* created by Mitchell Hurwitz, episode 13, Imagine Television, The Hurwitz Company, and Twentieth Century Fox Television, 2005, disc 4. DVD.

Viewed as an original television broadcast
"Beef Consomme." *Arrested Development*, created by Mitchell Hurwitz, season 1, episode 13, Imagine Television, The Hurwitz Company, and Twentieth Century Fox Television, 15 Feb. 2004.

Note: It doesn't seem to make much difference to me how you watch a particular episode, but MLA seems to value the medium (or "container") over the content in citation.

Television show without an episode title

Gameshows such as *Wheel of Fortune* or *Jeopardy* and variety shows such as *Saturday Night Live* do not feature episodes with individual titles. A citation would appear as follows:

Jeopardy! ABC, 25 Aug. 2021.
Saturday Night Live. Hosted by Elon Musk, season 46, episode 18, NBC, 8 May 2021.
Wheel of Fortune. TNT, 20 Dec. 2018.

YouTube

The title of a YouTube video is in quotes, and whoever uploaded the video is included in the citation. The "date" is when the video was uploaded.

In the spirit of self-promotion, here is one of my YouTube videos on the changes to the APA style manual from the 6th to 7th edition with a discussion group of students:

Hatala, Mark. "Top 10 Changes in the APA Style Manual - 6th to 7th Edition." *YouTube*, uploaded by Hatala Testing, 18 Nov. 2019, www.youtube.com/ watch??v=YDp9T4eCOJM.

Here's an example of a YouTube video without a designated author:

"The Role of the Witches in Macbeth." *YouTube*, uploaded by Rachel Vevers, 21 Apr. 2018, www.youtube.com/watch?v=A6s19XOxnj4.

Online Media - Social Media

E-mail and text messages

Although they are infrequently a part of an academic paper, I have personally cited emails from major figures in the field in my sabbatical applications. The person you've had the communication with should be cited, along with the day, month, and year that the communication took place. An example of a citation of an email I received from researcher Gordon Bell supporting my sabbatical application would be:

Bell, Gordon. E-mail to the author. 25 Aug. 2015.

If he had sent a text message instead, it would look like:

Bell, Gordon. Text message to the author. 25 Aug. 2015.

Facebook post

Social media posts are interesting because it makes a difference whether someone's account is "public" or not. If a Facebook post can only be accessed by someone who is a "friend," then putting in a link to that specific post might not be possible.

In keeping with non-political examples from famous people, here is a Facebook post from Barack Obama about MLK Day. His account is public, so anyone can see his posts. Here is how the post would be cited (note that you don't need to write the entire post, just a description of the post is fine):

Obama, Barack. "Thoughts on Dr. King's Letter from a Birmingham Jail." *Facebook*, 20 Jan. 2020, www.facebook.com/barackobama/posts/10157369262941749.

Note: This format should also be used for other social media sites like LinkedIn, Tumblr, etc.

Instagram photo

Why might someone use Instagram as a source? Because there ARE unique things to access via social media! For example, Phillip Zimbardo occasionally posts archival photos from his (in)famous Stanford Prison Experiment, such as the newspaper ad used to recruit student participants. If you're not familiar with his research, it's worth reading about.

Zimbardo, Phillip. Photo of Stanford Prison Experiment recruitment ad. *Instagram*, 17 Nov. 2015, www.instagram.com/p/-MVItMhow1.

Twitter

I value my sanity, so I stay off Twitter, but famous people have been known to tweet important information. You should retain the spelling and capitalization in a tweet, and reproduce any emojis (if possible). In order to avoid any political issues, here is an innocuous tweet from Barack Obama wishing his wife Michelle a happy birthday:

Obama, Barack [@BarackObama]. "In every scene, you are my star, @MichelleObama! Happy birthday baby!" *Twitter*, 15 Jan. 2020, twitter.com/BarackObama/status/1218174463046553600.

Online Media - Websites

The term "website" can cause confusion because it is so all-encompassing. For example, most journal articles are available online, and we cite them slightly differently depending on whether we used a physical print journal or an online database to access them. However, there are many sources which we can only access online, and that's mostly what I mean by "websites."

A consideration when using websites as sources is whether they would be judged to be "legitimate." There are times when information from a website may be the most up-to-date source for a particular topic. Information from sources like the Mayo Clinic (mayoclinic.org), the National Institute of Mental Health (nimh.nih.gov), and the Centers for Disease Control and Prevention (cdc.gov) are credible and cover a variety of topics. I also admit to having a soft spot for Science Blogs (scienceblogs.com) and the brilliant Cecil Adams at The Straight Dope (straightdope.com). .

Articles from websites can also be confusing because sometimes an article has an author, sometimes there is an organization that is the "author," and sometimes there's no author (or date) provided for the source. Each of these situations is presented below:

Website article with an individual author (or two)

The problem with websites is that unlike research journals, they are not peer-reviewed, and so any author can pretty much write anything, and who knows if it has any validity? However, many students will use information from websites to provide examples and anecdotes for their paper.

The citation for an article from a website contains the same "core elements" as any other source - author(s), title of the material (in quotes), source (or "publisher") of the material (in italics), the date the information was posted (if available), and retrieval information (the URL). One and two author examples follow:

One author:

McIntosh, James. "What is a Stroke? What Causes Strokes?" *Medical News Today*, 5 Sept. 2014, www.medicalnewstoday.com/articles/7624.php#treatment_ and_prevention.

De Silva, Matthew. "Need a New Year's Resolution? Here's What It's Like to Quit Facebook." *Quartz*, 31 Dec. 2019, www.qz.com/1776702/thinking-about-quitting-facebook-heres-what-its-like.

Two authors:

Paddock, Michael, and Connie Nordqvist. "What is Claustrophobia? What Causes Claustrophobia?" *Medical News Today*, 26 Sept. 2014, www.medicalnewstoday. com/articles/37062.php.

Website with no author or date

Sometimes people just throw things up on the web without any author or publication date, but don't despair! Remember that the works cited list is for the reader to be able to find a source you used in your paper, and so you should provide the information you have access to. For example, here's an authorless, undated general article on retiring to Costa Rica (a retirement goal of mine):

"Living in Costa Rica." *International Living*, www.internationalliving.com/countries/ costa-rica/live. Accessed 14 May 2021.

Note: The date the information was accessed is included in a citation when there is no date provided for when the information was posted or if the source has been altered or changed.

Website with a group author

The information from sources such as the Mayo Clinic (mayoclinic.org), the National Institute of Mental Health (nimh.nih.gov), and the Centers for Disease Control and Prevention (cdc.gov) usually comes from a "group author," meaning the organization itself. In the two examples, the "author" and "publisher" are the same organization, and so the "publisher" information can be omitted.

Centers for Disease Control and Prevention. "Stroke Facts." 6 Sept. 2017, www.cdc.gov /stroke/facts.

National Institute of Mental Health. "Post-Traumatic Stress Disorder (PTSD)." May 2019, http://www.nimh.nih.gov/health/topics/post-traumatic-stress-disorder-ptsd/ index.shtml.

Blog post

I find it interesting that "blog" derives from "web log" and that it's an acceptable source for a paper. The citation does not need to be identified as a blog post, and the "publisher" is in italics (like a journal!), followed by the URL:

Serdar, Kasey. "Female Body Image and the Mass Media: Perspectives on How
    Women Internalize the Ideal Beauty Standard." *The Myriad*, 16 July 2014,
    www.d-muntyan1215-dc.blogspot.com/2014/07/female-body-image-and-mass-
    media.

Comment on a website or blog

If there is any truism of our age, it is "Don't read the comments!" I can't imagine including an online comment from a website or blog in your paper, but that just reflects my own lack of imagination. Here's how to cite a user comment:

GlobalBizChick. Comment on "I Quit Facebook. Here's What Happened Next." *Lightspan
    Digital*, 21 Aug. 2014, 4:35 p.m., www.lightspandigital.com/blog/i_quit_
    facebook.

Note: The citation of a comment should include the time that it was posted.

The news website

Who reads a physical newspaper anymore? Many people get their news from the web, and the same basic format works for any "news" website you choose. Examples follow:

Brunner, Jeryl. "On the 110th Anniversary of Dr. Seuss's Birth His Quotes Continue to
    Inspire." *HuffPost*, 4 Mar. 2014, www.huffingtonpost.com/jeryl-brunner/on-the-
    100th-anniversary-_b_4891306.html.

Strickland, Ashley. "Some Mount Vesuvius Victims Suffered Slowly and One Victim's
    Brain Turned to Glass, New Research Says." *CNN*, 24 Jan. 2020, www.cnn.com
    /2020/01/23/world/mount-vesuvius-herculaneum-skeletons-scn/index.html.

Wikipedia

Have you heard of *Wikipedia*? If you haven't, you should check it out! *Wikipedia* is a good example that we are all familiar with. That said, there is a good chance that it will NOT be considered an acceptable source in a college paper, so check with your professor!

For some reason, while the 9th edition of the *MLA Handbook* provides multiple examples of how to cite things like "brochures and pamphlets," "billboards," and "museum wall text" (my personal favorite), it doesn't include a single example of a *Wikipedia* citation. However, leaving something out of the *MLA Handbook* doesn't mean it can't be cited, and *Wikipedia* is an online source like any other.

Wikipedia is constantly edited and updated, so entries can change from day to day. For this reason, the date that the entry was last modified is included in the citation. *Wikipedia* has an entry for "*MLA Handbook*." Let's use it as our example!

"*MLA Handbook*." *Wikipedia: The Free Encyclopedia*, Wikimedia Foundation, 29 Dec. 2020, en.wikipedia.org/wiki/MLA_Handbook.

All of the information is there. Since there is no "author" we just put the topic, and since it is a book it is in italics. We got the information from *Wikipedia*, which is in italics because it's a type of encyclopedia. The publisher is the Wikimedia Foundation. The December date is the day it was last modified and we provide a link to the web page. It's just that easy!

How would we do an in-text citation of a *Wikipedia* entry? Here's a sample sentence:

Writers have been given guidance on how to format papers ("*MLA Handbook*").

Miscellaneous

Although this is something of a "catch all" category, I wanted to include a few obscure citation examples that don't fit into any of the previous categories.

Conference presentation

Hatala, Mark. "Ready or Not: The 7th Edition of the Publication Manual." General poster session. National Institute on the Teaching of Psychology Conference, 5 Jan. 2020, Tradewinds Resort, St. Pete Beach, Florida.

Note: This is a poster I presented on the new edition of the APA style manual. The citation includes the name and date of the presentation, as well as the location of the conference.

Syllabus

Syllabus for Cognitive Science. Taught by Mark Hatala, spring 2021, Truman State University, Kirksville, Missouri.

Video game and Virtual Reality Experience

Red Dead Redemption. Rockstar Games, 18 May 2010.

MyndVR. *7 Miracles*. MyndVR app. Accessed 4 Aug. 2021.

Note: *Red Dead* is the last video game that I played from start to finish!

Odds and Ends

Citation management software - all your problems solved?

There's a technological solution for every problem, and the same is true for citation. I would feel remiss if I closed this book without discussing citation management software programs like Zotero, RefWorks, Mendeley, and about 20 others! Basically, after you scale the learning curve of how to use them, they correctly construct your citations in whatever format you choose - MLA, APA, Vancouver, Bratislavan, Chicago, and any other system in their database. So what's not to love? The learning curve.

If you're writing a few MLA style papers on different topics over the course of your high school and college career, I don't think that citation management software is worth the time. It's the equivalent of bringing a howitzer to kill a housefly. If you're a professor or graduate student writing multiple articles on the same topic for years though, it's the best thing since sliced bread, mostly because it organizes the hundreds (if not thousands) of sources you're likely to use over your academic writing career.

Inclusive language

Part of writing involves using specific, sensitive, acceptable, and appropriate terms for the people and groups you are writing about. Most gender-specific terms, such as "mankind" and "fireman," are easily reworded for gender neutrality as "humanity" and "firefighter." In terms of pronouns, MLA style endorses the use of the singular "they" as a generic third-person singular pronoun. For years, the use of the singular "they" was discouraged in academic writing as being non-specific, but in the past decade many publishers have embraced the term for purposes of inclusion, and so now it is a part of MLA style.

Terms for racial and ethnic identity follow the same logic of being specific, sensitive, and appropriate. In general, be as specific as you need to be, so if you are writing about people in Cuba, it is appropriate to refer to them as Cubans. If you are writing about people from Cuba who are living in the United States, they are Cuban Americans (no hyphen). While terms like *Latinx* are considered to be more inclusive, they are also nonspecific. In other writing style manuals (such as APA and Chicago), "Blacks" and "Whites" are considered to be proper nouns and are capitalized. According to MLA style, if a "dictionary gives both the capitalized and lowercased form as acceptable options - as many do for *black* and *Black*, for example - choose one and be consistent" (91).

Fonts and formatting

MLA style does NOT require writers to use only a few approved fonts, but does request that the font be "an easily readable typeface" and "between 11 and 13 points" (1). As a general rule, you'll be fine using a 12-point Times New Roman font for your paper. This might seem obvious, but you should pick a font and stick with it throughout the paper; DON'T change fonts between sections, paragraphs, etc.

MLA style requires that papers are double-spaced with 1 inch (2.54 cm) margins all around (top, bottom, left, right) the manuscript. The first line of each paragraph should be indented one-half inch from the left margin, so just use the "Tab" key. Also, your paper should be printed on white 8.5 x 11 inch paper. Whether you should print on a single side or both sides of the paper is up to your teacher. Most teachers require a header with your last name and the page number in the upper right-hand section of your paper. Finally, be sure to put one space (NOT two) after a period! The sample papers follow these formatting instructions.

Although some books on MLA style include a section (often running to 20-30 pages) on how to use Microsoft Word or Google Docs to set up a paper, I think this is a topic where "showing" through an instructional video is much better than trying to learn from screen shots inserted into a book. However, if you would like more guidance on how to use a word processing program, a very simple solution is to google "MLA style Google doc" or "MLA style MS Word" and you will immediately be presented with a number of templates and "fill-in-the-blank" sample papers, many of which are very good! The templates are usually distributed by educators who care about writing.

Headings and subheadings

While not usually used in essay-length papers, if you want a research paper to appear structured and organized, consider adding headings and suheadings! What's the difference between headings and subheadings? An example would be helpful:

Heading Level 1

Heading Level 2

Heading Level 3

As you can see, headings should be flush with the left margin of your paper. Putting a heading in **bold** or increasing the font size indicates that it is an important heading. A smaller font or the use of *italics* indicates a subheading. Don't use numbers or letters to identify headings, and if you are going to use them in your paper, have more than one for each level you use - so don't just have one Level 1 heading. In other words, if you're going to use headings in your paper, commit to using a number of them!

Numbers

One might say that there are a number of rules for writing about numbers. In general, words should be used to express numbers that can be written in just a word or two (one, fifteen, twenty-five, etc.) and numerals should be used for numbers that cannot (8.6, 152, 678, 3,245). Also, words should be used to indicate numbers when a number begins a sentence, a text heading, or a title.

Numerals should be used if you need to write about exact measurements (64 inches), abbreviations (4 lbs.), decimal fractions (3.14), years (2020), and exact units of money ($7.53). You should also use numerals in your works-cited list (vol. 3, no. 4).To complicate things, a combination of numerals and words should be used to write about large numbers (7.8 billion humans).

When you write about a range of numbers (such as page numbers in a citation), provide the complete second number (12-32 or 42-63) for numbers up to ninety-nine. For larger numbers, provide only the last two digits of the second number (106-07 or 421-44) unless you need to provide more digits to be clear about the range (397-405 or 1,321-464). A similar policy is followed when writing about ranges of years. For example, the First World War took place from 1914-17 and Albert Einstein lived from 1879-1955.

Works cited alphabetization

Many students have questions about what to do when different authors have the same last name (like Brown), similar last names (like Brown, Browne, and Browning), or no name at all. How is it all alphabetized in the references? Thankfully, it is not very difficult as long as you follow a few rules.

First, if a work has no author or editor, it should be alphabetized by the first important word of the title. In the examples below, the book *A Brown Pelican Marks the Spot* is alphabetized by the word "Brown" rather than "A" because "Brown" is the first meaningful word in the title.

In situations where multiple authors have the same last name, alphabetize by their first name. In the example below, Amanda Brown (with her fictional book about Taylor Swift) comes before Dan Brown (with his actual best-sellers).

What about situations where different authors have similar names, like Brown, Browne, and Browning? In cases like this, *nothing precedes something*, so an author named "Brown" would go before one named "Browne," and both would go before "Browning."

Three more notes about the mini-reference list below.

Dan Brown has three books on the list, and the books are alphabetized by title, so *Angels & Demons* is listed first. *The Da Vinci Code* is listed before *Digital Fortress* because we ignore articles like "The" (or "A" or "An") in a book title for purposes of alphabetization. Publication date is irrelevant when putting an author's books in a works cited list.

Since Dan Brown has three books, after the first listing of his name, each subsequent entry is just three hyphens followed by a period.

Finally, the book *A Brown Pelican Marks the Spot* appears before Jackson Browne's book because, as mentioned earlier, *nothing precedes something*.

It is hard to imagine a paper that would contain these particular sources (several of which I've invented), but it would be correctly alphabetized like this:

Brown, Amanda. *Taylor Swift: A Study in Genius*. Way Back Bay Books, 2018.
Brown, Dan. *Angels & Demons*. Pocket Books, 2000.
---. *The Da Vinci Code*. Doubleday, 2003.
---. *Digital Fortress*. St. Martin's Press, 1998.
A Brown Pelican Marks the Spot. Rocky Mountain High Press, 2012.
Browne, Jackson. *Still Running on Empty*. Rock Publishing, 1999.
Browning, Elizabeth Barrett. *Sonnets from the Portuguese: A Celebration of Love*.
　　St. Martin's Press, 2007.
Brownwood Sports Legends. Greentop Academic Press, 2010.

Quotations - Direct and block

This is an addendum to the section on in-text citations, and examples of direct and block quotations are presented there and in the sample papers at the end of this book.

Why would we use a direct quote? Sometimes we need to use a direct quote in a paper in order to get the wording exactly right; however, I strongly discourage my students from using direct quotes very frequently. Like block quotes (to be discussed momentarily), direct quotes can be used to pad out the length of a paper, and that can be pretty obvious to a professor. Some papers I've read are really just strings of direct quotes bound together with some intervening explanatory sentences. There have also been a number of times I've scratched my head and asked, "Why did they need to take a direct quote of THAT?!" Nothing shows an inability to paraphrase like the overuse of direct quotes.

A direct quotation must faithfully reproduce the spelling, wording, and punctuation of the original source material, so you shouldn't edit or change it. If you DO have to change the quote in some way, indicate the change using brackets or parentheses. Also, if your direct quotation contains a citation, include it in the quotation (after all, you're "faithfully reproducing" the original source), but don't add it to your works cited list: you're not using it as a source, the author of the quotation is.

Direct quotations are only appropriate if they take up four lines or less of your paper. If they're more than four lines, they should be incorporated into a block quotation, indented one-half inch from the left margin (see the second sample paper).

Plagiarism and academic dishonesty

The detection of plagiarism in student papers has gotten significantly easier over the past decade with the introduction of online tools such as TurnItIn.com and SafeAssign. Both of these tools compare a paper not just to every journal article in their databases, but to every website and every other paper ever submitted to the service. This means that you could get flagged for rewriting one of your OWN papers that you had turned in for another class.

However, most professors don't need a program to detect plagiarism. The "voice" of the paper just changes, or students begin using words and phrases that make it clear that they're copying down someone else's words or ideas. Students oftentimes don't understand that they've plagiarized if they've included a citation.

So how do you know when you've stepped over a line? Perhaps you're familiar with the "general rule" that's out there - if you use five identical words in a row without a direct quote citation, you've plagiarized. Well, maybe. It's not that difficult to paraphrase the writing of others; it just requires a little effort.

So let's take a look at an actual student paper on conformity. This was a "D" paper because it had numerous other issues (like the student misspelling the author they were plagiarizing). We can start out with the source they used, and then compare that to what the student wrote - the words that are plagiarized are in **bold**.

Source:
Natarajan, R. C. "Halo Effect in Trust." *IUP Journal of Management Research*, vol. 8, no. 1, Jan. 2009, pp. 26-59.

What the student wrote:
A study by RC Natarjan demonstrates about how a **principal may trust an agent due to either the latter's ability to carry out the task as competence trust** or to the perception **that the latter will not act in a manner detrimental to the relationship or the former (goodwill trust)**.

Natarajan source:

A principal may trust an agent either due to the latter's ability to carry out the task as desired (competence trust) or due to the perception that the latter will not act in a manner detrimental to the relationship of the former (goodwill trust).

A few comments. First, be sure to correctly spell the names of the authors you are plagiarizing. Second, in a 50 word sentence, 38 of the words are "identical words in a row" without a direct quote citation. While I would admit that the source material is not the clearest writing, a corrected, non-plagiarizing paraphrasing of the same source would read as follows:

A study by R. C. Natarajan demonstrates how a person might trust another person by either their ability to complete a task, called "competence trust," or their actions in building a relationship, called "goodwill trust" (28).

The author is cited correctly and the sentence has been put through the "de-jargoning machine" to distill the essence of what the researcher is trying to say, while also including the critical terms they discuss and the page number of the cited material.
Here's another example from the same paper, again with the words that are the same in bold:

According to Natarjan, **competence trust is formed through the principal's awareness and conviction regarding the agent's skills, financial ability and consistency in performance**.
Natarajan source:
For example, competence trust is formed through the principal's awareness and conviction regarding the agent's skills, financial ability and consistency in performance - thus providing reliability.

If anything, this is an even more egregious example because in a 23 word sentence, 20 of the words are "identical words in a row." The student didn't even correct for the improper lack of an Oxford (or serial) comma after the word "ability!"

Correction:
According to Natarajan, competence trust is created through "the principal's awareness and conviction regarding the agent's skills, financial ability and consistency in performance" (50).

In this case, a direct quote is appropriate because there's no really good way to paraphrase this sentence. As always, quotations should be used sparingly, but too many properly cited quotes is better than outright plagiarism.
I hope this section has made it evident that while often inadvertent, plagiarism is easily avoided by taking the time and effort to paraphrase a source or by simply using a direct quotation.

Sample student papers

It's one thing to understand the rules of MLA style and another to apply them in an actual paper. Therefore, this section includes two annotated student papers - one about a play and the other about a poem. These papers (like all the examples from student papers I've used in this book) are reproduced with the permission of the writers.

Have you ever seen one of those movies where at the beginning it says, "Based on true events?" That's kind of the deal with the sample papers too - although a student wrote each original paper, I've altered them in order to include a variety of different sources. Why? To illustrate how different sources appear when making in-text citations, as well as how they appear in the works cited list. Do I think that a student paper would have fourteen (14!) sources in a four page paper? It seems unlikely, yet both sample papers do!

My hope in this section is to reproduce the student/professor interaction that occurs when discussing writing and grades. No paper is "perfect," and I'm sure that there are still things wrong with both papers, but they serve as good examples of what an "A" paper looks like. I would also say that professors love "A" papers because they get all of the "little things" correct. The works cited page is done correctly. The in-text citations are frequent and appropriate. They include page numbers for citations when required. Your teachers know how much effort and dedication it takes to write an "A" paper, and since they are the quickest papers to grade, we're thankful for that too. I often find myself writing comments like "Interesting!" and "Good!" on "A" papers so that the students know that I've actually read the paper.

What tends to make "A" papers stand out isn't just the lack of problems, but the students' comfort with the subject matter. They are able to give an insightful take on the topic. They are able to find sources which compliment each other and can integrate those sources within the same paragraph (and often within the same sentence). Their command of the material allows them to notice the subtle differences in perspective between their sources. They just "get it" and are able to convey their knowledge to the reader in a way that is informative, clear, and interesting. It is the sophistication and command of the material which allows the "A" paper to stand out among the others.

I have included "comment bubbles" throughout the papers, but since I want to make some points about each page of the paper, I'll take that opportunity here. The only part of the paper missing "comment bubbles" is the works cited pages, and this is so that you have a "clean" copy of how things should be alphabetized and what they should look like. If you would like to see copies of the papers *without* comment bubbles, they are available at MLAcentral.com!

Female Identity in *Macbeth*

Page 1

Page 1 has your name, your teacher's name, the class you're enrolled in, and the date the assignment is due, all in the upper-left corner. This is an individual paper and so a title page is not necessary; however, if the paper is part of a group project you should make a title page with all of the authors listed alphabetically in the upper-left corner. On a group project title page, you would also center the title.

The upper-right corner has the page header, which is your last name and the page number. Some professors don't require a page header, and others do, so ask!

The title is centered and isn't in bold or underlined. The sample paper has *Macbeth* in italics because it is the name of the play that is being discussed.

The font used throughout the paper is 12-point Times New Roman (but other "legible" fonts between 11 and 13 points are acceptable), and the margins are 1 inch all around (top, bottom, left, and right).

Included on this page is an in-text citation of a direct quote from a YouTube video, an in-text citation of an article from *Wikipedia*, and an in-text citation of a direct quote from a website article without page numbers.

Page 2

The second page (and every subsequent page) also has a page header with the student's name and the page number.

This page begins with the most dubious source of all (outside of *Wikipedia*) - an article from a website (in fact, the British Broadcasting Company website, so technically a "news" website) with no date or author.

There is an endnote about the title "Thane of Cawdor." Endnotes are used to provide explanations (like what a "Thane" is) and are represented in the text by a superscripted number which corresponds to a number on the endnotes page. The second endnote on this page provides the dialog from the play where Lady Macbeth refers to her husband as a coward.

This page also provides examples of in-text citations from a website article and a TED Talk (from the TED website).

Page 3

The third page begins with an in-text citation of a direct quote from a physical print journal article (as opposed to a journal article accessed online).

The next comment bubble explains how to write an in-text citation of lines from a play in terms of the Act (1), Scene (5), and Lines (47-55). Note that a forward slash (/) is used to denote the line breaks in a play when quoted within the prose of a paper.

A third endnote explains the meaning of the phrase "man up" within the context of a specific live performance of *Macbeth* (which is also noted through an in-text citation).

The page ends with an in-text citation of a podcast.

Page 4

The fourth page begins with an example of an in-text citation from a TEDx Talk which was posted to YouTube. This is significant because there is a difference in the way a TED Talk appears in the works cited page based on the "container" it was accessed from (YouTube vs. the TED website). A small but important distinction.

The next in-text citation refers to an 1889 painting by John Singer Sargent of Lady Macbeth. I wanted to include an artwork viewed online (as opposed to "in person" or "in a book") in the paper too.

The third in-text citation is a direct quote from consecutive pages of a journal article which was accessed online. The format of the in-text citation is the same as for a physical journal article, but they are written up slightly differently on the works cited page. Again, another small but important distinction.

The paper ends with an in-text citation from a blog post, because why not?

Page 5 - Endnotes

The endnotes go on a separate page before the works cited page. The endnotes are numbered to correspond with the superscripted numbers from the paper, and indented.

Pages 6-7 - Works Cited

I've left these pages free of comment bubbles so that you can see how to write up each of the various sources. Each of them is genuine and not "made up" for purposes of illustration. They are, in abbreviated form:

Donkor - An article from a website
Gaze - A TED talk posted to YouTube
Gudenrath - A TED talk posted to the TED website
Jajji - A physical print journal article
Macbeth - A live performance of the play
"Macbeth Episode 2" - A podcast
Pine - A blog post
Ramsey - A journal article accessed online
Samuels - An article from a website without a date (so includes access date)
Sargent - A painting
Shakespeare - A physical print book of the play
"Shakespeare, Witchcraft and the Supernatural" - a website article with no date or author
Solomon - A YouTube video
"Three Witches" - A *Wikipedia* entry

Note: If you'd like to see a non-annotated (meaning no "comment bubbles') version of this paper, it's available at MLAcentral.com.

Hatala 1

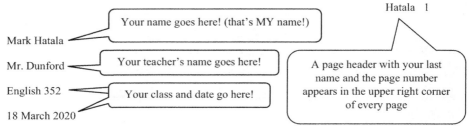

Mark Hatala

Mr. Dunford

English 352

18 March 2020

Your name goes here! (that's MY name!)

Your teacher's name goes here!

Your class and date go here!

A page header with your last name and the page number appears in the upper right corner of every page

Female Identity in *Macbeth*

Today, a reoccurring image of women as hidden and conniving beings in literature is not often seen. In current poems, plays, and novels, women are commonly seen as independent and strong heroines. However, in Shakespearean litera[ture] female

The title is centered

persona as being predominantly viewed in a "negative, helpless, or evil way" (Solomon 00:01:33-38). In regards to *Macbeth*, the main women in the play are portrayed as monstrous and crazy. The W[eird Sisters] rate ludicrous behavior, but though they

A YouTube in-text citation includes the hours, minutes, and seconds of the part containing the quotation you used

have unlikeable [qualities] ly clever and bold. They know how to manipulate peopl[e] ir unfavorable qualities, the females in Macbeth are intelligent and use their medieval womanly characteristics to their advantages by exemplifying determination and instigating the downfall of many men.

The Weird Sisters are the first characters introduced in the play and are also the first to foreshadow the demise of Macbeth ("Three Witches"). The three sisters are described as being ugly and wretched. They are the stereotypical wi[tches].

A *Wikipedia* in-text citation (but check with your teacher about whether Wikipedia is acceptable to use as a source)

Since Shakespeare gives them their hideous ima[ge]

H[...]

m[...]

A direct quote from a website which does not have page numbers does not require a parenthetical citation

Unlike other women in Scotland who are wives and [...] l or influence of men. Deborah Samuels states, "The witches in Macbeth fly in the [face of] the patriarchal society. Early in the play, the witches seem to have no such male superior." The sisters show the first indication of female authority in the play, and not only are they self reliant, but they are highly intelligent. The witches pr[ovi]de

Macbeth and Banquo with prophecies which have hidden and ambiguous meani[ng]...

example, later in the play when Macbeth returns to the witche[s]...

remain king of Scotland, the witches give him new prophecies that do provide comfort for him.

One of the prophecies says that he will remain king until the woods of Birnam march on

Dunsinane castle. Another says that no man born from a woman will ever conquer Macbeth

("Shakespeare, Witchcraft and the Supernatural"). Thinking that these are all impossible

happenings, Macbeth feels satisfied th[at] ... him.

However, the witches are incredibly cleve[r] ... [e]ach of their

prophecies. They know that Malcolm's army will use the woods' leaves and branches as

camouflage and literally march onto the castle to destroy Macbeth. The sisters also know that

Macduff was born after his mother had already died, making him born from a dead woman, not a

living one.

   Although they have a ne[...] Weird Sisters are

intelligent and conniving. They ultimately did instigate Macbeth['s dow]nfall from the very first

prophecy they gave him which foretold that he would be Thane of Cawdor[1] and then king, but

they knew that[...] [wou]ld eventually lead to his

death. Whethe[r...] [belie]f in prophecies, the Weird

Sisters used their Shakespearian qualities to help ... [the] tragic end of Macbeth.

[Ma]cbeth is also portrayed as "harsh and crazy" (Donkor). She

co[...] [tellin]g him that he is cowardly and unmanly[2], which were

serious insults for medieval men (Gudenrath). Along with h[...] the one

who initiates the murder plan of Duncan that brings suffering to all of Scotland. Like her

Annotations:

- The page header appears on every page
- This is a good example of an article on a website without an author or a date
- Endnotes are used for explanations that might get in the way of the flow of the paper
- A direct quote from a website which does not have page numbers does not require a parenthetical citation
- This is a TED-Ed Talk about insults in Shakespeare
- Another endnote

husband, she becomes [···] the king. She begins to develop a very dark personality. [···] beth is a witch herself. Jajji asserts, "Lady Macbeth is ambitious, but her aim [···] no barriers, moral or temporal. Her speech leaves no one in doubt that she is the fourth sister to the witches" (234). Though Lady Macb[···]ants is to not be restricted by the female gender norm[···] Lady Macbeth proclaims, "Come, you spirits / That t[···] And fill me from the crown to the toe top-full / Of direst cruelty [···] me to my woman's breasts / And take my milk for gall [···] urd'ring ministers..." (1.5.47-55). Lady Macbeth wishe[···]at she is able to carry out the murder. She fears that if h[···] he will not be able to properly help kill Duncan since she b[···]spect.

How[···] he murder, he becomes nervous and ashamed of wha[···] all men are consistently brave and fearless. With his unsteadiness, Lady Macbeth tells him to "man up[3]" ("Macbeth") and when he is unable to return to Duncan's body to place the dagger, Lady Macbeth d[···] him [···]

As the play moves forward, she continues to cov[···] start to arise. Though Lady Macbeth is taking on more of the husbandry role, people still solely associate her with feminine qualities. Men in the castle want to shield Lady Macbeth from the horrors she has witnessed because they believe she is too frail. However, none of them realize that she has planned the murder herself and [···] he is a female, men automatically overlook any qualities she pos[···] at may be considered bold or manly. Although she may be slightly crazy, murde[···], and sometimes nervous, she is even more meticulous, brave, and forceful ("Macbeth Episode 2"). While Lady Macbeth is portrayed in

---

Annotation callouts:

- Since the author's name appears in the sentence, the parenthetical citation of the page number appears directly after the quotation
- The in-text citation of lines from a play include the Act (1), Scene (5), and Lines (47-55)
- A forward slash (/) is used to denote the line breaks in a play when quoted within the prose of a paper
- This endnote requires explanation, as it is ironic in reference to a specific performance of *Macbeth*
- This in-text citation is specific to a particular performance of *Macbeth*
- This in-text citation is a podcast

Macbeth as an evil woman, and ultimately drives herself mad and kills herself, her determination

and courage put a [   ] en in Shakespeare's writing.

Lady Macbet[h   ] than not, receive negative recognition.

> This is a TEDx Talk which was posted to YouTube

The theme of presentin[g   ...n] as either incapable or evil is not unique only in *Macbeth*.

Numerous other wo[rks] [b]y William Shakespeare also demonstrate woman as having these same

characteristics (Gaze). However, in this play specifically, women are able to defy some of their

gender stereotypes, even if not in the [   ] y well that

Macbeth will fall for their tricky prop[   ] [o]wing that

Macbeth is a fool for believing them in the [   ] Had Macbeth not been so infatuated with

the idea of becoming king, his demi[se   ...] [wou]ld never have happened. Though the witches told him

many predictions, Macbeth [...on]ly brought death and deception upon himself, with the assistance

> This in-text citation refers to Sargent's 1889 painting of Lady Macbeth crowning herself (viewed online)

of Lady Macbeth (Sargent). Jarold Ramsey asserts, "the more Macbeth is driven to pursue what

he and Lady Macbeth call manliness, the less[...t]s nearly

all claims on the race itself, and his vaunted [   ]

meaningless" (286-287). [Until her own death ...] husband

> An in-text quotation from a journal article includes the consecutive pages where it appears in that source

for not living up to his manly status. Whether she pushed him too hard to achieve a gender role,

she definitely pushed him too hard to be courageous until she herself was more manly than

Macbeth (Pine). However, men and wom[en alike continued to view her as gentle and] dainty,

without recognizing her conniving and b[...] [e]xhibiting

her dominant personality over her husba[nd   ...] [h]es to

> Since this is Pine's idea, she is given attribution for it in the in-text citation. Also, this is from a blog post.

overcome in the medieval era, the Weird Sisters and Lady Macbeth demonstrate that the negative

personas of women do not overshadow their forceful and clever characteristics.

44

Hatala 5

Notes

1. Thane of Cawdor is a peerage title in Scotland. Co... Campbell is the current 7th Earl

of Cawdor, and 26th Thane of Cawdor.

2. Lady Macbeth's exact quote is "Wouldst thou have that / Which thou esteem'st the

ornament of life, / And lie a coward in thine own esteem / Letting 'I dare not' wait upon 'I

would' / Like the poor cat i' th' adage" (1.7.41-45).

3. The 13 Nov. 2019 performance of *Macbeth* at the James G. Severns Theater featured

genderbent casting (sometimes known as "cross... der" casting), so a male performer (Max

Richards) played Lady Macbeth and a female per... Courtney Klein) played Macbeth,

making the statement ironic.

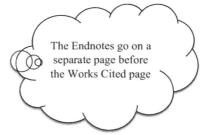

"Notes" is centered

The in-text citation shows that the quote
is from Act 1, Scene 7, Lines 41-45.

The Endnotes go on a
separate page before
the Works Cited page

Works Cited

Donkor, Michael. "Character Analysis: Lady Macbeth." *British Library*, 19 May 2017,

    www.bl.uk/shakespeare/articles/character-lady-macbeth.

Gaze, Christopher. "Shakespeare is Everywhere." *YouTube*, uploaded by TEDx, 21 Mar.

    2012, www.youtube.com/watch?v=LsESSyMnwmU.

Gudenrath, April. "Insults by Shakespeare." *TED*, Apr. 2012, www.ted.com/talks/april_

    gudenrath_insults_by_shakespeare?language=ent-217355.

Jajji, M. Ayub. "A Feminist Reading of Shakespearean Tragedies: Frailty, Thy Name is

    Woman." *Pakistan Journal of Commerce and Social Sciences*, vol. 8, no. 1, 2014. pp. 228-

    37.

"Macbeth Episode 2 – Lady Macbeth." *GCSE English RevisionPod* from Podtail, 1 Apr. 2019,

    www.podtail.com/en/podcast/gcse-english-revisionpod/macbeth-episode-2-lady-macbeth.

Pine, Sarah Appleton. "The Tragedy of Lady Macbeth." *Ploughshares*, 2 Mar. 2020,

    www.blog.pshares.org/index.php/the-tragedy-of-lady/macbeth.

Ramsey, Jarold. "The Perversion of Manliness in Macbeth." *Studies in English Literature, 1500-

    1900*, vol. 13, no. 2, 1973, pp. 285-300. *JSTOR*, www.jstor.org/stable449740.

Samuels, Deborah. "Macbeth and Issues of Gender." *Yale National Initiative*.

    www.teachers.yale.edu/curriculum/viewer/initiative_07.01.03. Accessed 13 Mar. 2020.

Sargent, John Singer. *Ellen Terry as Lady Macbeth*. 1889. Tate Britain, www.tate.org.uk/art/

    artworks/sargent-ellen-terry-as-lady-macbeth-n02053.

Shakespeare, William. *Macbeth*. Directed by David Charles Goyette, 13 Nov. 2019,

    James G. Severns Theater, Kirksville, Missouri.

46

Shakespeare, William. *Macbeth (Folger Shakespeare Library)*. Edited by Barbara Mowat and
    Paul Werstine, Simon & Schuster, 2013.

"Shakespeare, Witchcraft and the Supernatural." *BBC*, www.bbc.co.uk/teach/shakespeare-
    witchcraft-and-the-supernatural/zvfyd6f. Accessed 8 Mar. 2020.

Solomon, Bersabhe. "Feminist Analysis of Macbeth." *YouTube*, 8 Apr. 2012,
    www.youtube.com/watch?v=xTMGxR5dSsg.

"Three Witches." *Wikipedia: The Free Encyclopedia*, 5 May 2018, Wikimedia Foundation,
    en.wikipedia.org/wiki/Three_Witches.

Reminiscence

Page 1

As in the previous student paper, the first page has your name, your teacher's name, the class you're enrolled in, and the date the assignment is due, all in the upper-left corner. A title page is not necessary; however, if the paper is part of a group project you should include a title page with all of the authors listed alphabetically in the upper-left corner. On a group project title page, you would also center the title.

The upper-right corner has the page header, which is your last name and the page number. Some professors don't require a page header, and others do, so ask!

The title is centered and isn't in bold or underlined.

The font used throughout the paper is 12-point Times New Roman (but other "legible" fonts between 11 and 13 points are acceptable), and the margins are 1 inch all around (top, bottom, left, and right).

Included on this page is a tweet by the poet about his early life, an in-text citation of a direct quote from a YouTube video, and a one-page work (a newspaper review) that doesn't require a page number in the citation.

Page 2

The second page (and every subsequent page) also has a page header with the student's name and the page number.

This page begins with an example of a block quotation of a poem (lines 1-6). The next comment bubble explains how to write an in-text citation of lines from a poem. Note that a forward slash (/) is used to denote the line breaks in a poem. The page concludes with a direct quote from a website which does not include page numbers (and therefore does not have page numbers in the parenthetical citation).

Page 3

The third page begins with an example of the writer's own analysis, which doesn't need citation, and is followed by an example of a definition from a dictionary. The page concludes with an in-text citation of a website.

Page 4

The fourth page begins with an example of an in-text citation from a website. It concludes with a final paragraph which summarizes the major points of the paper, and includes an example of the use of the singular "they."

Pages 5-6 - Works Cited

I've left these pages free of comment bubbles so that you can see how to write up each of the various sources. Each of them is genuine and not "made up" for purposes of illustration. They are, in abbreviated form:

Alexie - A tweet
Alexie - A physical print journal page
"Big Think Interview" - A YouTube video

Caffrey - An article from a website
Clement - An article from a website
"Guilt, *N*. (3)" - A dictionary (the third entry definition)
Klinkenborg - Newspaper review accessed online
MasterClass staff - An article from a website
"Repetition" - An article from a website with no author or date (so includes access date)
Ross - A journal article accessed online
Thompson - An article from a website
Ullman - A physical print journal article
Walsh - Newspaper review accessed online
Weinberger - A physical print newspaper review (single page)

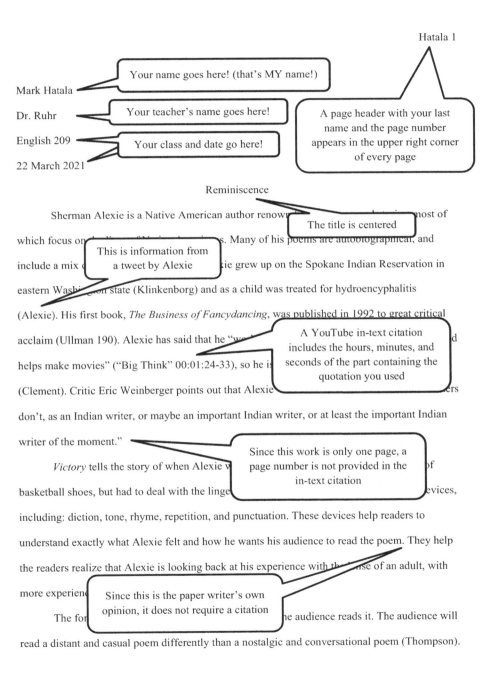

Hatala 1

Mark Hatala

Your name goes here! (that's MY name!)

Dr. Ruhr

Your teacher's name goes here!

English 209

Your class and date go here!

22 March 2021

A page header with your last name and the page number appears in the upper right corner of every page

Reminiscence

Sherman Alexie is a Native American author renow~~~~~~~~~~~~~~~~~~most of which focus o~~~~~~~~~~~~~~~s. Many of his poems are autobiographical, and include a mix o~~~~~~~~~~kie grew up on the Spokane Indian Reservation in eastern Wash~~~~~~on state (Klinkenborg) and as a child was treated for hydroencyphalitis (Alexie). His first book, *The Business of Fancydancing*, was published in 1992 to great critical acclaim (Ullman 190). Alexie has said that he "w~~~~~~~~~~~~~~~~d helps make movies" ("Big Think" 00:01:24-33), so he is~~~~~~~~~~~(Clement). Critic Eric Weinberger points out that Alexie~~~~~~~~~~~~~rs don't, as an Indian writer, or maybe an important Indian writer, or at least the important Indian writer of the moment."

The title is centered

This is information from a tweet by Alexie

A YouTube in-text citation includes the hours, minutes, and seconds of the part containing the quotation you used

Victory tells the story of when Alexie v~~~~~~~~~~~~of basketball shoes, but had to deal with the linge~~~~~~~~~~~evices, including: diction, tone, rhyme, repetition, and punctuation. These devices help readers to understand exactly what Alexie felt and how he wants his audience to read the poem. They help the readers realize that Alexie is looking back at his experience with th~~~~se of an adult, with more experien~~~~~~~~~~~~~~~~~~~~~~

Since this work is only one page, a page number is not provided in the in-text citation

The fo~~~~~~~~~~~~~~~~~~~~~~~he audience reads it. The audience will read a distant and casual poem differently than a nostalgic and conversational poem (Thompson).

Since this is the paper writer's own opinion, it does not require a citation

50

Alexie's *Victory* has a clear, somber to[ne] [Block quotations of a poem should be indented and preserve the line breaks of the original poem] xie is telling a story from his past, it is not in the typi[cal] ut the poem creates a sense of sadness or longing; he i[s tell]ing a happy story. His poem starts out especially melancholy, say[ing]:

> When I was twelve, I shoplifted a pair
>
> Of basketball shoes. We could not afford
>
> Them otherwise. But when I tied them on,
>
> I found that I couldn't hit a shot.
>
> [Identify the line numbers of the poem at the end of the block quote] ff the rim, I felt
>
> (lines 1-6)

The words "we could not afford them otherwise" stick out as being notably somber, as a twelve-year-old is aware that his family is impoverished and cannot even afford a pair of shoes. Similarly, "... I threw those cursed Nikes / In the river and hoped that was good / Enough for God" (lines 9-11) reveals Alexi[e's] ous feelings, particularly in the word "cursed." The tone thr[oughout] allowing the readers to relate to Alexie's emotions. In a [A forward slash (/) is used to denote the line breaks in a poem when quoted within the prose of a paper] ps the [word]s su[ch] come from a twelve-yea[r-old] [A direct quote from a website which does not have page numbers does not require a parenthetical citation] [lin]e 6). A stereotypi[cal] ankles! O, blisters the size / Of dimes and quarters!" (lines 15-16). This matur[e ton] stands out because the audience knows Alexie is twelve years old at the time the story takes [pla]ce, and reinforces critics estimation of him as "a bold writer who goes straight for the aorta" (Walsh). These words, in association with the overall tone, remind readers that Alexie is not a twelve year old, but in fact, an adult looking back with new knowledge and experiences.

51

Hatala 3

The act[ual] ... [autho]rs, including but not limited to: rhyme, repetiti[on] ... [lik]ely comes from rhyme and repetition. The rhyme in Alexie's poem does not have a sp[ecific] rhyme scheme. The rhymes are inserted throughout the poem, preventing the poem from sounding forced. In the first stanza, Alexie rhymes "not" and "shot" in two different lines, tying the lines together (lines 2, 4). "Distraught" and "caught" are also rhymed within the same line (line 8). Rhymes help poems flow smoothly

> Since this is the paper writer's own opinion, it does not require a citation

and connec[ts] ... The word flow in *Victory* is natural and linked ... [us]e of repetition in his poem. Like rhyming, repetition ... [re]aders connect different parts of the poem together, in addition to creating emphasis ("Repetition"). For instance, Alexie repeats "guilt" three times in a row in line 6. The repetition creates emphasis on the feeling of guilt; guilt is a very strong emotion can be defined as "a feeling of deserving blame for offenses" ("Guilt"). Lines 6, 7, 14, and 15 all contain the word "O." Repeating this word ... the

> The paper writer is paraphrasing the source work, and so requires a citation

two together. It also emphasizes what com[es] ... [a]nd bloody heels and toes (lines 6, 14). Because ... [rhym]es and stanzas in *Victory* are tied together, again reminding the readers that Alexie is writing as an adult and is able to tell the story with precision and in the most aesthetically interesting way possible.

> This is a definition from the Merriam-Webster online dictionary

It is very important for an author to write a poem in a way that the audience understands how to read it. A common way to show the ideal pace of a poem is through punctuation. Alexie uses a lot of enjambment in *Victo[ry]* ... line to the next (MasterClass staff). Lin[e] ... [sent]ence continues onto the next line, which also happens to be the next stanza. Adding a period at the end of the stanza would have created a pause rather than a smooth transition. Alexie also uses end-stopping

> The paper writer is paraphrasing the source work definition of "enjambment" and so requires a citation

to create a pause in the flow of reading (MasterClass staff). He endstops lines 4, 14, 18, and 24, the last line of the poem, for instance. Putting a [period at] the last line in the poem gives the end a finality. Alexie also uses commas t[...] Only guilt, guilt, guilt," for example, utilizes c[...] [...]er to p[...]nctuation with short sentences speeds up the pace at[...] hand, longer sentences with less punctuation will slow down the pace. Because [...] able to manipulate the speed at which the audience reads his poem, it is a reminder that he is an adult who is capable of emphasizing very specific parts of a large text.

> The paper writer is paraphrasing the source work definition of "end-stopping" and so requires a citation

> Since this is the paper writer's own opinion, it does not require a citation

    Victory continues to be an influential poem today because it combines diction, tone, rhyme, repetition, and punctuation to retell [...] from childhood with a new, adult lense. The audience can read the poem in the [...] he had to learn. Reading Alexie's poem all[...]ences with a more mature lens, as Alexie himself did. It is important to understand that one will look at an experience differently depending on their age.

> The final paragraph summarizes the major points of the paper for the reader

> The use of the singular "they" is acceptable in MLA style

Works Cited

Alexie, Sherman [@Sherman_A1966]. "In the beginning of my book I talk about how I was

   born with too much water in my head. Basically, I had too much cetebral spinal fluid in

   my skull." *Twitter*, 6 Mar. 2018, twitter.com/sherman_a1966?lang=en.

---. "Victory." *Prairie Schooner*, vol. 89, no. 4, Winter 2015, p.16.

"Big Think Interview With Sherman Alexie." *YouTube*, uploaded by Big Think, 23 Apr. 2012,

   www.youtube.com/watch?v=kJmRaLUcVUB.

Caffrey, Angelique. "Importance of Rhythm and Flow." *Explore Writing*, 14 Aug. 2018,

   www.explorewriting.co.uk/rythmflowhaiku.html.

Clement, Nick. "Smoke Signals Fim's Effect 20 Years Later Topic of Discussion." *Variety*, 26

   Sept. 2018, www.variety.com/2018/film/news/smoke-signals-25-years-later-1202959185.

"Guilt, *N.* (3)." *Merriam-Webster*, 2021, www.merriam-webster.com/dictionary/guilt.

Klinkenborg, Verlyn. "America at the Crossroads: Life on the Spokane Reservation: *Reservation

   Blues* by Sherman Alexie." *Los Angeles Times*, 18 June 1995, www.latimes.com/

   archives/la-xpm-1995-06-18-bk-14204-story.html.

MasterClass staff. "End Stops and Enjambment in Poetry: Definitions and Examples." *Master

   Class*, 19 Mar. 2021, www.masterclass.com/articles/end-stops-and-enjambment-in-

   poetry.

"Repetition." *Poets.org*, www.poets.org/glossary/repetition. Accessed 15 Mar. 2021.

Ross, Stephen. "Ragged and Rugged Formalism." *The Oxonian Review*, issue 9.2, 4 May 2009,

   www.oxonianreview.org/wp/ragged-and-rugged-formalism.

Thompson, Van. "What Are the Characteristics of Conversation Poems?" *Pen and the Pad*, 21

   Feb. 2019, www.penandthepad.com/characteristics-conversation-poems-22871.html.

54

Ullman, Leslie. "Betrayals and Boundaries: A Question of Boundaries." *The Kenyon Review*,

vol. 15, no. 3, 1993, pp. 182-196.

Walsh, S. Kirk. "Time-Traveling Lessons for a Teenager on the Verge." *The New York Times*, 25

Apr. 2007, www.nytimes.com/2007/04/25/books/25wals.html.

Weinberger, Eric. "Off the Reservation." *The New York Times*, 15 June 2003, p. G13.

One Last Thing . . .

I want to thank you for using this book and giving me the opportunity to help you improve your writing and understanding of MLA style. If you enjoyed this book and found it useful, I would appreciate you leaving positive feedback in whatever venue that you choose. Your experience will help others make a decision on whether to choose this book, so feedback is important.

I'm used to student evaluations at the end of every semester, so if you didn't find this book helpful or feel that it's lacking information you would want to see, I would ask you to send me an email to let me know what I can do to improve it. I'm easy to find online - I'm the Mark Hatala who is a college professor, and NOT the one who is the dentist or the golf pro.

I will close by saying that I'm honored to be even a small part of your educational experience. Everyone has things that they can teach in this life, and most things are learned outside of any classroom. I put lots of YouTube videos up about the topics that interest me and the classes I teach, so mostly videos on writing, romantic relationships, and time travel. The opportunity to teach people I will never have the chance to have in a physical classroom means a lot to me, and so does decision to use this book. Thank you!

Index

Made in the USA
Las Vegas, NV
09 August 2022

52995845R00036